Introduction

Whenever I send a poem (my very best can do not to wave it off, as if it were leaving home. I might even blow a kiss, or give an encouraging thumbs up as it looks back all vulnerable and paper-thin from the letterbox slot, or most likely the computer screen, and then – whoosh it's gone. All you can do then is wait with hope in your heart, knowing it's a cruel world out there and the odds are stacked. My feeling is, that if you can sit alone with your own poem and be amazed it came out of you, you – then its worth is already assured, whatever any judge might think. Which brings me to…..

We all have our preferences and prejudices as to what poetry we enjoy. I tried to at least temper my biases and assess each poem on its merits. I want to be convinced the poet felt it, and then does the language excite me? I put heart before head every time, but if the language isn't right, then I'm afraid whatever else the poem has is lost to me. I want to be surprised and delighted by a poem, to be made to think afresh. I'm please to say I found plenty in the heart of the poems I read. Those that rose to the top, were those that in my opinion best accomplished their intent to pierce my armour. I am grateful to all of the poems and their writers though, for making the task of judging such an enjoyable and difficult one.

Martin Figura

First Prize

Memory House

When nouns – proper and common –
began to go, she remembered
Giordano Bruno,
his memory theatres
by means of which an orator
might recall the propositions
of a speech, and place sentences
in key positions such as a pediment,
architrave or column within
an imagined theatre.
                         She would use
her childhood home
which she could not shake off
and adorn it with entities
and situations
of greater fragility –

fireplace, kitchen sink, flagstones
in the larder; coal cellar,
woodshed, the kitchen
window where the cat
came in. The bookcase
on the upstairs landing –

she would tie what she wanted
to remember to these solid
locations as some tie prayers
and wishes to a tree, making the
fastening firm with a double bow.
There. The name of a long ago lover
tied to the mantelpiece, and there
the town in Sardinia where someone
– was it she? – fell over and grazed
her knee as a child might do
and the woman from the cake shop
ran out with a chair and a slice
of a tart made with apricots
ranged beautifully
like roof tiles.

Elizabeth Cook

GEORGE CRABBE POETRY COMPETITION 2020

**Prize-Winning and Commended Poems
Adjudicated by Martin Figura**

Inaugurated in 1954 – the bicentenary of the birth of George Crabbe

Published by
Suffolk Poetry Society
Registered Charity No. 1162298

Copyright of the poems remains with the poets

Suffolk Poetry Society
All rights reserved

ISBN: 978-0-9511789-6-6

Further copies may be obtained
from the Shop on the
Suffolk Poetry Society website
suffolkpoetrysociety.org

Contents
Introduction — Martin Figura   1

Prize-Winning Poems
Memory House — Elizabeth Cook   2
Frank's World — Jane Henderson   3/4
Lament for a Lewis Crofter-Man — Mike Bannister   5

Highly Commended Poems
Critical Care — David Healey   6
Young Birds — Tim Lenton   7

Commended Poems in alphabetical order by poet
Halcyon — Sally Baker   8
she is on her way — Alexandra Davis   9
Isle of Man Internees — Caroline Gilfillan   10
Lichen Seen through a Magnifying Glass — Caroline Gilfillan   11
Paced — David Healey   12
Return to Southwold — Christopher James   13
The Brickie's Prayer — Rob Lock   14
Harvesttime — Oliver Nelmes   15
Learning How To Fix a Lamp — Kennedy Osborne   16/17
Weaving fresh weft over old warp — Fran Reader   18
Latin Lovers — Margaret Seymour   19
Titian puts down his paintbrush and picks up his guitar — Roger West   20
That Perfect Feeling — Richard Whiting   21

Adjudicator's Comment
First Prize   22
Second/Third Prize   23
Highly Commended   24
Commended   25
Winners and Adjudicators 1998-2019   26
Suffolk Poetry Society   27
George Crabbe — James Knox Whittet   28/29

A special thanks to Fairweather Law Ltd for sponsoring the prize money
Competition Secretary

Second Prize
Frank's World

Frank was a knitted boy: plain and purl,
with a spare hand that attached
a harmonica to the slot of his mouth
which he then assumed like a silver grin,

harping through it a language of his own.
His face was pure purl, the curve of ear,
the tilt of brow, the prow of lips kiss-pursed.
Frank's mother had cast him off the row

like unwanted stitches, and Frank had felt
himself so cast, falling with weight yet silently
with the gravity of a tightly spun ball of,
for example, Aran, there being a slight

bounce and a degree of unravelling.
Frank then grew independently, breeding
his own ideas like stick insects and wheeling
them around on the velvet nap of caterpillars.

Frank was sweater and shorts, scratchy
grey above stocking-stitch knees, long
frayed from forays into the hedge where
the thrush nested. Frank's spare hand

had plumbed the thrush's nest, fingered its
rough weft, felt the yarn in its rotundity.
Otherwise he stood with his toes curled
around stones in the soft silt of the river bed,

the cloudy water knee high and dough warm,
tightening his toe grip on the stones,
and all the time sliding the mouth harp.
He wanted to banish the frightful images

of cauliflower that kept creeping into his head,
the vegetable having been served to him
once for school dinner. He had fled down
the lane away from school, back to his bed

at Grand-daddy's house. In his dreams
the heavily textured white curd pulsed
like a huge brain, then broke in half,
exuding a glaucous substance from its parts.

All Frank wanted to taste was the wood,
the metal of the harmonica, he blowing
and sucking at the honeycomb grid of it,
meting out his vernacular of stickleback,

blackbird's egg and Grand-daddy's pipesmoke.
Grand-daddy was braces and clay-smeared spade,
drawing long-necked tear-inducing leeks
from the sod of his allotment.

Somehow Frank had a notion that blind, black
men played blues on harmonicas, so Frank
shut his eyes when he struck up his mouth harp
and focussed on the hue of the blackbird's egg.

Jane Henderson

Third Prize
Lament for a Lewis Crofter-Man (i.m. Kenny Kennedy of Orasaigh 1943-2016)

Further... as far as... back of the north wind
    we hanker after recollection's warp,
    where the last crags tumble, chill dark
    and terrible to the underworld.

Prince, whale-man and weaver, lone voyager,
    we came to re-discover you.

Malin to Fair Isle: twelve windless days,
    all mute, no shout carries, no echo tells;
    the sharp steel barb of that, salt rust and sore
    drives deep.

Un-rippling, at Orasaigh waves gleam
    green and silver, mirror those mornings
    we'd put out on the ebb tide, trusting
    the flood to bring us home, lines coiled, fish box full.

You taught us the sea; hidden skerries
    lee shore, whistling squalls, a cable parted,
    a readiness for danger.

Life-log of a crofter-man: Handsome youth
    quits the Long Isle, earns his spurs
    where the whale-fish blow, about the Weddell Sea;
    then he's a tanker-hand
        Thames Humber Tyne and Forth.

In the high woods of Moray, he finds his own
    pearl beyond price, brings her home,
    builds a small Ithaca, clear spring, rough land
    dry boat, iron loom; they work, weave tweed,
    raise a constellation of four lambent stars.

Restless, down all the seasons and the years,
    our quiet Odysseus, is busy at the brim
    of the sea, a godly man, each repeated
    labour a ritual in itself, a prayer almost;
    fish of the tide, cloth of the loom
    peat of the moor, stag from the hill.

Sage thoughts, uttered in the old tongue,
    soft and slow; he would provide.

Boatman, friend, hero and hunter, sleep sound
    in your dark school among the stones
    of Gravir, place of kings.

Mike Bannister

Highly Commended Poems

Critical Care

He phoned 111 after three days of fever,
said he couldn't breathe, and barely
remembered going in the ambulance.
*Likes to be called Ray   Ethnicity: mixed
Religion: Methodist   Supports Arsenal.*

It's been three weeks now, just hearing
gowns rustling, machines bleeping,
suction and trolleys wheeled to and fro,
visors and goggles leaning over him
and speech muffled by tight masks.

His family wave and blow kisses
from an iPad and show him the birds
that are visiting his garden feeder.
*Prefers apple juice to orange, coffee to tea
though has lost both taste and smell.*

One nurse stays in a Portakabin to avoid
taking the virus home. Another came out
of retirement to work in a Covid ward.
Luke writes 'Mary' on the front of her gown
and Mary writes 'Luke' on the front of his.

Nothing in life prepared him for this:
the widening gaps, the absences
and faces on screens that are far away.
*Likes talking about June, his late wife,
and the holidays they had in The Lakes.*

Today, his breathing and 'sats' are better.
They're helping him walk to a window
where he can see blue sky and trees
in full leaf, neither framed nor virtual,
imagined or described anymore, but real.

David Healey

Young Birds

Light flashes in the hedge
as young birds
free from the fields
taste the edges of their new world

then come to feed from our fingers:
sunlight pierces their wings
and the puzzle of leaves and branches
as we watch,

remembering Columba
the holy dove
and the flames of light
that settled on him, filled his house

full of love and secrets,
consuming the dry, tender land.

Tim Lenton

Commended Poems in alphabetical order of poet

Halcyon
Detail from 'The Garden of Earthly Delights' by Hieronymus Bosch

I'm not to scale with the man who sits at my feet
holding a woman's face as if to kiss her
or confess a sin. My beak frames the scene –
a blade, closed scissors, a missile about to launch.
My breast is the velvet curtain at the edge of his stage.

Two men in black and white inspect my tail,
their heads just visible in the dark.
My scarlet claw is the size of a human face.
It rests on a mallard's back; we're all on board,
flying over the man in love with a barn owl.

We birds all turn our beaks to the temple,
prepare to fly in formation over the crowds.
My body is also the world – a dark blue sky
over sea, summer lightning on the horizon.
A sandy beach runs down from the forest

of island I carry on my wing. There, flung out
on the waves, is the light of a solitary fisherman.

Sally Baker

she is on her way.

his body moves with the sudden strength and flex of youth. sculpture returns to flesh. he has lifted two rusted garden chairs from the back of the house out to the front garden. they will conduct their reunion in tableau like ancient Greek theatre. no thresholds will be broached today. they will sit two metres apart within the circling arms of the privet. they are in an Austen novel. he has placed her chair farthest from the bins. they will gaze and grin at each other like bookends shielding a strange story. theirs. they will co-exist in three dimensions for the first time in eleven weeks. she will bring cupcakes upturned by speedbumps. her hair will be longer and her laughter will burst and fall like joyous ashes around them. the duet of their conversation will be like summer has arrived. the poise of their bodies will be breath-taking.

Alexandra Davis

Isle of Man Internees

Stuffed into the tall terraces of Hutchinson Square
they ripped up lino to score into prints, concocted paint
from clay, brick dust and dribbles of sardine oil.
Marjan Rawicz sampled eleven pianos and when one
fell to pieces artists grabbed the panels, carted them away.

Kurt Schwitters painted the badge and cap, the kind face
of prison guard Edward Driscoll on a tea chest panel,
and hid his own epilepsy and gloom
under a cloak of Dadaist performance and barks,
sleeping in a room ripe with putrid porridge sculptures.

Hundreds of them lugged chairs to the modest rooms
and bumpy lawns of the Lecture House
to listen to mathematicians, artists, musicians,

a lion tamer who could pick dandelions with a swish
of his lasso. They squashed into a bedroom to watch
Of Mice and Men and snigger at Romeo and Julian.

Some baked, sewed, cooked kippers, hung washing
on the fence. Many worked on the island's farms.
But come nightfall they were all behind the wire
in rooms thick with male sweat, breath and snores.

More than a thousand were locked up here:
Hitler's Degenerates, Communists and Jews,
exiles who'd fled to Britain from the knock on the door,
the shattered windows and guarded ghettoes,
the blows, blood, spittle and cattle trucks.

Now they were Enemy Aliens, Jerries, Wops,
after Churchill barked *Collar the lot.*

Caroline Gilfillan

Lichen seen through a Magnifying Glass

Through the bulge of the glass
I peer at the slate wall
and enter a miniature desert of
scree and black splurge.

And on a larch tree I locate
a pelt of green that was a companion
to William and Dorothy
as they squelched
from Grasmere to Ambleside
to collect the post. Close up
it smells of wood and warmth –
a survivor from a time
when mammoths trampled
the temperate rain forest.

I'm looking for an acid-yellow lichen –
the one I saw on pavements and walls
between the purple prettiness of aubretia
when I cycled to the beach
along the quiet roads that led to shingle.

But it's absent
from this soft, moist place –
another thing I've left behind
like the whistle of the pressure cooker,
the LP of the Emperor concerto, the skittish cat
giving her dusty belly to the sun.

Caroline Gilfillan

Paced

Cocooned under a blue drape,
I feared the worst, wondering
if I'd ever return for a cup of tea
and worrying you'd be scared
it had taken so long, our dog Polly
left alone and unfed at home,
your phone storing missed calls.

There was much more rummaging
around than I ever expected.
Firstly, the pacemaker generator
wouldn't fit below my collarbone.
Then, one of the leads, they tried
to get round a difficult bend,
they couldn't screw into my heart.

Successful at last, the effects
of my second dose of Fentanyl
kicked in. Eric, my cardiac nurse,
played piano music by Einaudi.
Angels in pyjamas were wheeling
me to an empty slot in the sky.
Faces smiled down from above.

You were waiting, as if I'd gone
off somewhere and you'd spent
hours looking for me, only to find
I was in the next room and hadn't
told you. Nothing new, then.
Under the sheets, I felt you
searching for my missed beats.

David Healey

Return to Southwold
*George Orwell came to Southwold in 1921 beginning
an association with the town that lasted for 20 years*
               Ronald Binns

His train pushes east like a line of prose,
leaving ligatures of steam trailing in the trees.
Each field is a page from his life: a village
green becomes the cricket pitch at Wellington.
A toppled windmill is the ruin of a temple
in Syriam. As he fills his pipe, he believes he
can see an elephant staggering into the ashes.
At a crossing, he glimpses himself as a younger
man in a shabby suit and philtrum moustache,
clutching a posy of peonies for Jacintha.
He hears the trill of a bicycle bell as if to signal
the end of a thought. At Walberswick, he hears
the tapping of rain and then sees the lighthouse
at Southwold like a pen spilling a pool of lilac ink.

Christopher James

The Brickie's Prayer

Lord of the monk, the Sussex and the double Flemish bond,
the stretcher, header, soldier and sailor,
the shiner and the rowlock too,
Lord of the half bat, three quarter bat
and occasional queen closer,
Lord of the single leaf wall, of all cavities and ties,
let this building be good for three centuries or more.
Grant it sympathetic beds and borders,
dignified neighbours and vistas that remain unspoiled.
May it never give rise to subsidence or other Buildings claims,
and, Lord, forgive any who here bind themselves in husbandry,
any here committing to housewifery,
should they call it theirs while they are passing through.

Rob Lock

Harvesttime

Between two tanned leather palms
he grinds long ears with sturdy calm,
then brings cupped hands, and blows the chaff
that hides the measure of the crop.

For unworked hands, the spike will scratch,
it buffs and sands my pale small grip.
The unthreshed field tickles against
small ankles, that march the borders
a pace and stride behind my father.

The clutch creaks and jerks up,
with sudden same-old jolt that creeps
the rust greened tractor through the yard

across the field, along Chelmer's
banks, fit to burst and flood it all
seeping, through the dirt beneath
the roots - suffusing up stems
into their heads, into my hands.

Oliver Nelmes

Learning how to fix a lamp

See, that's one thing you'll learn:
keep everything.

Thumbs wishing for calluses usher in a new fuse.

A lot of these are what Jim made,
turned them on a lathe.
Motions to a hammer hanging up,
its handle unfinished for good reason.
The soft glamour of the wood
outstanding from graphite walls
and dense plastic bees.

He's one person I do miss.

We try the lamp, nothing.
I guess I'm just lucky I've got this stuff.
Screwdriver set is prised from boxes
the handles glimmer the same
understated uniform -
And I still use it sometimes.

The flat, level head pirouettes
coaxing aged metals from their sheds.

I love doing this stuff,
but with both jobs,
paying off the cards,
I don't have the time.

Copper in my palm glints
I wait to return it
keep my fingers unfurled
to breathe its rusted mist.

His sister called me in tears.
Said she didn't know who else to talk to.
I was a bit cut up myself.
Vocal chords clear dust
chiseled groove in the lamp's base,
   This is where the wire sits.

Pieces from my hand slot back
home, snug.
   I don't really talk about him much.
   But I don't half think about him.

In goes the plug again,
and our breath grows golden
mingling above the bulb.

Kennedy Osborne

Working fresh weft over old warp

I saved a tapestry from moth destruction the way one saves a soul
Louise Bourgeois, diary entry, November 2 1995

Warp – strange name.
I'll make it my word-of-the-day

to please Maman.
She'll give me a linen backdrop of taut threads

exposed by greedy moths
with no thought for beauty –

a free-for-all in dust-making decay –
a lost face, a missing fleur-de-lis.

For her I'll restore the missing weft with woollen threads –
tannin fixed, to madder-red, weld-yellow and woad-blue.

Over-and-over I'll let the soft threads
stroke my fingers – colour retell the story.

When I've finished I'll sing – if sound will come –
a song for the warp I've buried.

Fran Reader

Latin Lovers

Salvador Dali gets around: one moment
he's attached to a wall can-opener
next he's back on the washing-machine.

In the drawer he lies on the Sigmund Freud
mouse mat. Its syncretic charisma
challenges his own: both finger-puppet

and fridge magnet, he's an archetype
of dissociative identity disorder. He's drawn
to Frieda Kahlo. You find them back-

to-back, their black velour craniums
conjoined. It takes two hands to separate them.
She looks good in red, flowers in her hair.

He's chic in high white collar, striped tie.
Her eyebrows respond to his signature
moustache. They will not kiss.

Margaret Seymour

Titian puts down his paint brush and picks up his guitar

mussel shell tuna fin cuttlefish ink
pyrite powder azurite zinc

cerulean celadon cadet and celeste
crows wing gull feather robin egg ravens nest

midnight diamond byzantine slate
imperial prussian palatinate

the heart of the spark at the heart of the flame
ferrocyanide blood in the vein

kingfisher starfish silver lake and capri
peacock periwinkle anemone

indigo aqua ultramarine
french fig and damson and aubergine

cornflour columbine lapis lazuli
indian ocean mediterranean sea

ice cap polar night magnetic ash
rock salt and cobalt thunderbolt flash

berber and breton ceylon and chartreuse
jesuit sacristan la vierge douleureuse

turquoise and teal tiffany true
woke up this morning, baby, I had all of those blues
yeah, woke up this morning, baby, I had all of those blues
all of those blues
all of those blues

Roger West

That Perfect Feeling*

The news bulletin disappears,
its breath smelling of apocalypse.
Even the sky seems sad,
as if the seasons themselves
were suspended.

And then a brimstone flitters
across a verge. Sun pulls
apart the clouds
as the first real warmth of Spring
settles on my face.

Blue sky reveals two buzzards
drawing circles, one around the other,
cracking mews across the valley.
The radio sends out a length of guitar,
to join them

the musician
seeming to follow their flight,
picking out their progress along the fret,
and they to mirror his mood,
a synchronicity.

The song is over. Two distant buzzards
melt into cloud, the radio falls silent.
I was dreaming, attending the only festival
I shall catch this year, up there, suspended
briefly by a chord.

Richard Whiting

* from 'Like A Hurricane' by Neil Young

Adjudicator's Comments
Martin Figura

First Prize

Memory House – *Elizabeth Cook*

'Memory House' handles a tender subject that's been written of countless times, with great sensitivity and intelligence. The poem looks a little strange on the page, but the risks it takes make perfect sense when read out loud. It had my attention from its arresting first line. I've often found the opening of a poem is rather like a theatre set, and here it's literally the case. The concept of a *memory theatre* provides the approach to tackle the loss of words (and therefore memory) – and straight away places a seemingly contradictory and interesting premise by having the protagonist remember something, that might help her deal with this. The device convincingly ties abstract memories of *greater fragility* to *solid locations*. Through this, we are taken back to the protagonist's childhood home and totemic first memories which *she could not shake off.* These are humble things presented without sentiment. I like that they are tied with *a double bow*, ironically something poems are sometimes accused of doing too neatly. No such thing happen here, the poem ends delicately with *apricots / ranged beautifully / like roof tiles* – a striking simile, full of metaphorical possibilities, as is the poem, leaving plenty for our own imaginations to enjoy and be moved by.

Second Prize

Frank's World – *Jane Henderson*

'Frank's World' also steps off with an arresting image and idea – F*rank was a knitted boy: plain and purl*…. Who wouldn't want to know more? This poem tumbles along, taking us from one original and striking image to the next. It's dressed like a steady poem safely buttoned up in its twelve unrhymed four-line stanzas, yet unravels like a runaway ball of wool pursued by a kitten. It achieves this through skilful enjambment, critically between many of the stanzas. Indeed, in some stanzas like the 2nd, the stanza has seemingly finished its business, …*prow of lips-pursed*. But no, there's a 4th line that runs right on into the next stanza. Frank's World is a playful poem; we are in Frank's woolly head and what a delightfully peculiar place it is. We travel through rivers and hedges; are stalked by school dinner B-movie cauliflower as we flee to *Grand daddys' house* and pipe smoke. We end with Frank comforted by his *mouth harp…..the hue of the blackbird's egg*. A sweet mystery of an ending as beguiling as the poem's opening line. A terrific poem, that came within a kitten's whisker of winning.

Third Prize

Lament for a Lewis Crofter – *Mike Bannister*

The odd language and syntax of this poem got my attention. It beautifully evokes time and place – again from the very first line: *Further….as far as….back of the north wind.* We are led into a chill dark underworld. Along the Crofter-Man's life journey lies the fickleness of the weather and geography, his formative travels and love. Love calls back to the opening stanza's Odyssean mythical underworld. Together with his unnamed 'Helen', he raises a constellation of four lambent stars. The poem mines the epic scale of a humble life lived, allowing us to feel the primal urgency of an existence we may have, during indulgent moments, yearned for from our armchairs.

Highly Commended

Critical Care – David Healey

'Critical Care' is a Covid-19 poem, of which unsurprisingly there was no shortage. People turn to poetry at times such as these. To write successfully of something immediate affecting everyone is beyond difficult. This poem succeeds by telling the simplest of stories, that cuts to the very quick of our fears and sadly in many cases – experiences. The bare facts are told with detached precision and without artifice. It is this straightforward honesty that goes right through us – no-one is called a 'hero' but *Luke writes 'Mary' on the front of her gown and Mary writes 'Luke' on the front of his*. No amount of emotive or dramatic language will ever cut as deep as the routine of that act and the others in this poem. The writer of this poem trusts the reader to have a heart beating in their chest. No lessons are meted out or fingers pointed, yet we learn all we need to know.

Young Birds – *Tim Lenton*

Once I'd reminded myself about Columba, I found myself on Iona. Somehow judging a Suffolk competition, I was with 'Young Birds' on a Scottish Island again. The seemingly simple octet of this unrhymed sonnet speaks of fledglings finding their wings *to taste the edges of their new world*. The opening line of the sextet and hinge of the sonnet is only two words: *remembering Columba*. Those two words are the key to the poem, not only to the rest of the poem, but recontextualising the opening octet. St Columba was driven out of 6th Century Ireland to become Scotland's first asylum seeker. The story of St Columba is a treasure trove, but the poem does not burden itself with exposition. Instead it uses it and the associated metaphor to lightly evoke the resultant human cargo of today's world's ills. It wishes for a …*house/ full of love and secrets / consuming the dry and tender land.*

Commended

I can vouch that all the **Commended** poems are well worth reading more than once or twice. 'Harvesttime' will grab you with its musicality; 'Return to Southwold' will cleverly conjure George Orwell; 'Learning how to fix a lamp' will teach you there is much pleasure to be had in that task; in 'Latin Lovers' Salvador Dali and Frida Kahlo are drawn to each other and a number of household appliances; 'The Brickie's Prayer' asks its many Lords for nothing less than the bestowing of domestic bliss for generations to come; 'Halcyon' walks us through the many peculiar delights of Hieronymus Bosch's Garden of Earthly Delights; 'Isle of Man Internees' tells of how art gives hope and purpose; 'Working fresh weft over old warp' restores souls and sings in celebration; 'Lichen seen through a Magnifying Glass' looks so closely, we find ourselves in the company of the Wordsworths amongst mammoth-trampled flora and fauna; 'she is on her way' brings hope and sexual tension in the guise of cupcakes upturned by speedbumps as lockdown is eased; 'Titian puts down his paintbrush and picks up his guitar' sings what else, but the blues – all of those blues; 'Paced' is the anxious interlude in the story of a heart; and what better way to finish than with 'The Perfect Feeling' and its resonant last line *I shall catch this year, up there, suspended briefly by a chord.*

Winners and Adjudicators 1998 - 2019

Year	First Prize	Adjudicator
2019	Christopher James	Tiffany Atkinson
2018	Caroline Price	André Mangeot
2017	Jim Green	Esther Morgan
2016	Pamela Job	Moniza Ali
2015	Caroline Gilfillan	Robert Seatter
2014	David Healey	Gregory Warren Wilson
2013	Pamela Job	James Knox Whittet
2012	Caroline Gilfillan	Kenneth Steven
2011	James Knox Whittet	Elaine Feinstein
2010	Gill Napier	Gareth Calway
2009	Mike Bannister	Clive Scott
2008	James Knox Whittet	Graham Fawcett
2007	Laura Helyer	Georges Szirtes
2006	Andrew Frolish	Neil Powell
		Andrea Holland
2005	James Knox Whittet	Danielle Hope
2004	James Knox Whittet	David Holliday
2003	Rosemary Merry	Alison Chisholm
2002	Elizabeth Bracken	Rodney Pybus
2001	Ros Cogan	Anne Beresford
2000	Helen Burke	Anthony Thwaite
		Ann Thwaite
1999	Rupert Malin	John Mole
		Julian Stannard
1998	Julian Stannard	Judith Kazantzis

For all First Prize Winners and Adjudicators from the competition's inauguration in 1954 up to 1997 please see the Suffolk Poetry Society website

Suffolk Poetry Society

Suffolk Poetry Society (SPS), a registered charity (no 1162298), began as *The Suffolk Poetry Club* in 1928 and became Suffolk Poetry Society in 1952, making it the oldest poetry society in England. Members come from East Anglia and beyond.

SPS Poetry Events occur throughout the year (sometimes in collaboration with musicians and singers) for all who love to hear, read or write poetry.

Events include:

- The annual Festival of Suffolk Poetry, which takes place in Stowmarket each year and includes workshops, open mic, readings by well known poets, and showcases the work of local Café Poets.
- An annual tea party for members only, usually with a guest speaker.
- Desert Island Poems featuring a well-known guest selecting their favourite poems as a way of sharing anecdotes from their life.
- An awards ceremony for the annual George Crabbe Poetry Competition.
- Other events where members perform their own work, sometimes with a local or historical theme and with music as well as words.
- Workshops

The George Crabbe Poetry Competition held annually since 1954 for members of SPS and poets born, educated, living or working in Suffolk.

SPS Newsletters sent by email to members to draw attention to all up and coming events in the county and wider afield.

SPS Website providing information about poetic events in the county: suffolkpoetrysociety.org.uk

SPS Portfolio: a postal poetry workshop. Poems are circulated once a month for other participants to read and make constructive comments.

Twelve Rivers is the magazine of SPS and is currently printed twice a year.

Café Poets: SPS supports activities of Suffolk based Café Poets by providing links to their websites, showcasing their poetry at the annual festival, and publicising their events through the newsletter.

In 2020 many of the above activities were run virutally online due to the Covid-19 pandemic. .

SPS is a Stanza of the Poetry Society

GEORGE CRABBE

George Crabbe was born in 1754 in the then impoverished village of Aldeburgh where his father pursued that most unpopular of professions: a tax collector. George developed a great love of poetry as a child but at the age of fourteen, he was apprenticed to a local doctor, medicine being viewed as a much more likely source of regular income than writing verses. However, he gained little medical knowledge in Aldeburgh so he changed masters and moved to Woodbridge where he met his future wife, Sarah Elmy, who was to become a life-long encourager of her husband's writing and helped him to overcome the inevitable rejections which writing poetry involves. Like many major poets throughout history, Crabbe decided to self-publish his first collection of poems which met with little attention.

Having completed his medical training, he recklessly decided to abandon a medical career and devote his life to poetry. In 1780, he travelled to London in the hope of gaining a foothold in the literary establishment. After months of virtual destitution, he wrote a pleading letter to the highly influential statesman and philosopher, Edmund Burke who, admiring Crabbe's writing, helped him have his long poem, *The Library* published. It was also Burke who perceived Crabbe's religious sensibility and persuaded Crabbe to enter the church and he was ordained as a clergyman and eventually appointed as chaplain to the Duke of Rutland at Belvoir Castle in Leicestershire.

Crabbe's best known works are the long narrative poems, *The Village*, published in 1783 and *The Borough* in 1810. Crabbe was a great admirer of Alexander Pope and, like Pope, he preferred to write in rhyming couplets. *The Borough* is based on Crabbe's early life in Aldeburgh and is written in a series of twenty-four letters, each illustrating a different aspect of village life which is depicted in a realistic and unromantic manner, in sharp contrast to the pastoral tradition of English verse. The character of Peter Grimes who appears in Letter XXII inspired the opera by Benjamin Britten which is regarded as one of the greatest operas of the twentieth century. However, the Peter Grimes of the opera is a more sympathetic figure than in the poem where he is portrayed as a sadistic and pitiless man.
Through elegant rhyming couplets, Crabbe depicts a shocking world of poverty and

brutality relieved only by the beauties of the natural world. Indeed, Crabbe was a minute observer of nature and wrote a study of insects. At Trowbridge, many of his poems were written while sitting under a mulberry tree in the rectory gardens.

Like many respectable figures of his time, Crabbe imbibed opium throughout his entire adult life with no apparent ill effects although one cannot know what effect this had on his perceptions and sensibility.

Crabbe gained many notable admirers in his lifetime: he was said to be Jane Austen's favourite poet; he had a profound influence on the poetry and prose of Thomas Hardy. Lord Byron justly said of him that *he was nature's sternest painter yet the best*.

Ironically, the very qualities which made his poetry so popular in his time: the lengthy narratives and the rhyming couplets have made him too little read in our time. Those who take the trouble to dip into his poetry would be impressed and often moved by his depictions of the harsh realities of the life of the great majority of people in the England of his day. He is one of those rare poets who have given a voice to the voiceless. He writes about the people and the world in which he inhabited with deep compassion and consummate craftsmanship.

George Crabbe died in 1832 and is buried in the sanctuary of St. James's Church in Trowbridge and there is a memorial to him in the north wall of the chancel. There is also a monument to him in Aldeburgh. For over sixty years, the Suffolk Poetry Society has played an admirable role in helping to preserve the memory of Suffolk's greatest poet.

Although one associates Crabbe with long narratives, one of his most memorable and touching poems is a brief lyric written in honour of his wife, Sarah, who never recovered her mental health after the death of their son, Edmund when he was aged just six. For the remaining seventeen years of her life, Crabbe devotedly looked after Sarah and summarised a lifetime of love with the following four simple but heartfelt lines, *A Marriage Ring* moulded out of gold verbal nuggets:

THE ring, so worn as you behold,
So thin, so pale, is yet of gold:
The passion such it was to prove –
Worn with life's care, love yet was love.

James Knox Whittet